W9-BAI-689

Cooking Pot

Rosie and the Big Bad Bear

"Where are you going, Rosie?" asked Mom.

"Out to play in the sandbox," said Rosie.

"Look out for Bosco, the big bad bear," said Mom.

"I'm not scared of Bosco," said Rosie. "I'm too smart for *him*."

Out went Rosie. Along came Bosco,
the big bad bear.

"Hello, Rosie," said Bosco.
"What are you doing?"

"Playing," said Rosie.

"Can I play, too?" asked Bosco.

"Yes," said Rosie.

They played in the sandbox together.
Bosco made holes, and Rosie made hills.

I'm too tough for Rosie.

I'm too tough for Bosco.

Then Bosco said, "I know another game we can play. We can play the game where a big bad bear eats up a little girl." He growled and showed his sharp teeth.

But Rosie wasn't scared.
"I know a better game," she said.
"We could play the game where a little girl eats up a big bad bear."

"Little girls don't eat bears," said Bosco.

"Some do," said Rosie. *She* growled, too.

Bosco looked a little bit scared.

I eat bear every day.

"I love bear."

"I eat bear for breakfast," said Rosie,
"and bear for lunch." She went on growling
and showed *her* sharp teeth.
Bosco looked scared.

5

"I have roast bear
for Sunday dinner,"
said Rosie, "and I have
bear sandwiches
in my school lunch.
Sometimes I have fried bear
with french fries."
She growled some more.

6

Bosco was looking *very* scared by now.
"I have to go, Rosie," he said.
"I think my mother is calling me."

"We haven't played the game yet,"
said Rosie, still growling to herself.

"Another day," said Bosco,
and he ran away down the street.

I've escaped.

Rosie sat in the sandbox, smiling.
"I was too smart for Bosco,"
she said.

Lala-she-BO

Man went out one morning,
Lala-she-BO
To hunt the yellow lion.
Lala-she-BO
He hunted by the river.
Lala-she-BO
He hunted in a thorn tree.
Lala-she-BO
He called out to the lion,
Lala-she-BO
"Come here and I will kill you."
Lala-she-BO

Yellow lion gave a roar.
Lala-she-BO
Yellow lion showed its teeth.
Lala-she-BO
Man dropped his spear and ran.
Lala-she-BO
Said he'd hunt another day.
Lala-she-BO

9

The Hobyahs

Once upon a time,
a little old man and a little old woman
lived in a house made of corn stalks.
They had a little dog named Turpie.

In the dark forest nearby, lived the hobyahs.

One night,
when the little old man
and the little old woman
were fast asleep,
out from the dark forest
came the hobyahs.

They crept around the
house and peeped in
at the windows.

"Hobyah! Hobyah! Hobyah!" they cried.
"Pull down the corn stalks.
Gobble up the little old man.
Carry off the little old woman."

Little dog Turpie barked and barked.
He barked so loudly that the hobyahs
ran away.

The little old man woke up and said,
"That little dog Turpie barks so much
I cannot sleep nor slumber.
In the morning, I will tie up his tail."
And he did.

He tied up little dog Turpie's tail
to stop him from barking.

The next night, out from the dark forest
came the hobyahs.

They crept around the house
and peeped in at the windows.

"Hobyah! Hobyah! Hobyah!" they cried.
"Pull down the corn stalks.
Gobble up the little old man.
Carry off the little old woman."

Little dog Turpie barked and barked.
He barked so loudly that the hobyahs
ran away.

The little old man woke up and said,
"That little dog Turpie barks so much
I cannot sleep nor slumber.
In the morning, I'll tie up his legs."

And he did. He tied up little dog Turpie's
legs to stop him from barking.

The next night,
out from the dark forest
came the hobyahs.
They crept around the house
and peeped in at the windows.

"Hobyah! Hobyah! Hobyah!" they cried.
"Pull down the corn stalks.
Gobble up the little old man.
Carry off the little old woman."

Little dog Turpie barked and barked.
He barked so loudly that the hobyahs
ran away.

The little old man woke up and said,
"That little dog Turpie barks so much
I cannot sleep nor slumber.
In the morning, I will tie up his mouth."

And he did. He tied up
little dog Turpie's mouth
to stop him from barking.

So little dog Turpie
couldn't bark at all.

The next night,
out from the dark forest
came the hobyahs.
They crept around the house
and peeped in at the windows.

"Hobyah! Hobyah! Hobyah!" they cried.
"Pull down the corn stalks.
Gobble up the little old man.
Carry off the little old woman."

Little dog Turpie tried to bark.
He tried and tried, but he couldn't.

17

The hobyahs pulled down the cornstalks.
They ran into the house, crying,
"Where's that little old man?"

But the little old man
had woken up
and was hiding
under the bed,
so the hobyahs
did not find him.

18

They *did* find the little old woman.
They tied her up in their bag
and carried her off to their house
in the dark forest.

They hung up the bag, and every hobyah
knocked on the top of it, and cried,
"Look me!   Look me!"
Then they went to bed.

When the hobyahs had gone away,
the little old man crept out from under
the bed and said, "Now I know why
little dog Turpie was barking."
And he untied Turpie right away.

Little dog Turpie *was* pleased.
He ran around, barking and barking.
Then off he went to the hobyahs' house.

He found the little old woman in the bag.
He let her out, and she ran home as fast
as she could.

Then little dog Turpie
crept into the bag himself.

When the hobyahs woke up, every hobyah
knocked on the top of the bag and cried,
"Look me! Look me!"

Out jumped little dog Turpie.

He gobbled up every one of those hobyahs.
Every one.

And that is why there are no hobyahs today.

Michael Finnegan

a song

There was an old man named Michael Finnegan.
He grew whiskers on his chin-again.
The wind came out and blew them in again.
Poor old Michael Finnegan—begin again.

There was an old man named
Michael Finnegan.
Had some boots made out of tin-again.
When he walked, he made a din-again.
Poor old Michael Finnegan—begin again.

22

There was an old man named Michael Finnegan.
He grew fat, and he grew thin again.
Got big wrinkles in his skin-again.
Poor old Michael Finnegan—begin again.

There was an old man named
    Michael Finnegan.
Played a tune on his violin-again.
Lost his place and had to begin again.
Poor old Michael Finnegan.

Hello! What's Your Name?

My name is Dan Dooly.
I come from Kalgoorlie.
I work in a gold mine down there.
And, every day,
when I walk down the street,
all the people I meet
say, *Hello! What's your name?*
And I say,
My name is Dan Dooly.
I come from Kalgoorlie.
I work in a gold mine down there.
And, every day,
when I walk down the street,
all the people I meet
say, *Hello! What's your name?*

My name is Dan Dooly.
I come from Kalgoorlie.
I work in a gold mine down there.
And, every day,
when I walk down the street,
all the people I meet
say, *Hello! What's your name?*
And I say,
My name is Dan Dooly.
I come from Kalgoorlie.
I work in a gold mine down there.
And, every day,
when I walk down the street,
all the people I meet
say, *Hello! What's your name?*
And I say,

The Tale of the Cook

a play

● **Captain** ● **Number One** ● **Number Three**

● **Number Two**

● **Crew**

● **Cook**

● **Number One:**
The submarine's got a hole in it.

● **Captain:**
A hole in it?

● **Number One:**
Yes, sir. A hole in it.

26

Crew:
The water's coming in,
and we can't swim.
Please, sir, what shall we do?

Captain:
Number One,
put your nose
in the hole.
Stop the leak.
Save the submarine.

Number One:
Yes, sir. Yes, sir.
Just like this, sir.
Ouch! My nose is cold.

27

Number Two:
The hole is
getting bigger.

Captain:
Bigger?

Number Two:
Yes, sir.   Bigger.

Crew:
Sir, the water's coming in,
and we can't swim.
What shall we do?

Captain:
Number Two, put your
hand in the hole.
Stop the leak.
Save the submarine.

Number Two:
Yes, sir.   Yes, sir.
Just like this, sir.
Ouch!   My hand is cold.

28

Number Tree:
The hole is
getting bigger.

Captain:
Bigger?

Number Three:
Yes, sir. Bigger.

Crew:
Sir, the water's coming in,
and we can't swim.
What shall we do?

Captain:
Number Three,
put your foot
in the hole.
Stop the leak.
Save the submarine.

Number Three:
Yes, sir. Yes, sir.
Just like this, sir.
Ouch! My foot is cold.

Cook:
The hole is
getting bigger.

Captain:
Bigger?

Cook:
Yes, sir. Bigger.

Crew:
Sir, the water's coming in, and we can't swim. What shall we do?

Captain:
Cook, you will sit in the hole.

Cook:
Did you say me, sir?

Captain:
I did.

Cook:
And did you say *sit*, sir?

Captain:
Yes, Cook, I did.

●**Cook:**

Yes, sir. Yes, sir.
Just like this, sir.
Ouch! The water's cold.

32

Captain:
Cook has saved the submarine.
For more than a week
he stopped the leak
by sitting in the hole.

Crew:
Three cheers for Cook.
Hip-hip-hooray!
Hip-hip-hooray!
Hip-hip-hooray!

Cook:
And now
my tale is told.

Home Cooking

Little Mr. Norridge
Made himself some porridge.
Made himself a lovely loaf
Of brown, crusty bread.

"If I had a brother,
I could bake him up another."
Then he went and baked another,
Which he ate himself instead.

Fly

Silly fly thought he'd lie
Flat on his back
On the railway track.
Great big train came rushing by.
Squishy, squashy, silly fly.

The Runaways

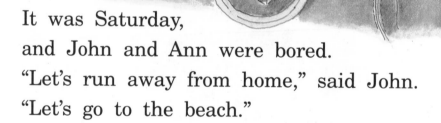

It was Saturday,
and John and Ann were bored.
"Let's run away from home," said John.
"Let's go to the beach."

"All right," said Ann.
"But we'd better tell Mom first."

Mom was mopping the kitchen floor.
"Hey, Mom," said John, "we're going
to run away."

"Run away?" said Mom. "Where?"

"Not far," said Ann. "Just to the beach."

"We get bored staying at home," said John.

"*You* get bored!" cried Mom.
"What about *me*?"

"You can come with us," said Ann.

"Yippee!" yelled Mom,
and she threw down the mop.
"I'll get some sausages."
Then she said, "Let's ask Dad, too."

Dad was working on the car.
He was grumbling.
"I'm sick of this car," he said.
"I've been working on it all morning,
and it still won't go."

"Forget it," said Mom. "Come with us.
We're running away from home."

"We're all bored," John said, "so we're
going to the beach."

"Fantastic!" cried Dad. "I'll come, too.
We can stay all night.
I'll get the sleeping bags."

So Mom and Dad and the children ran away
to the beach. Well, they didn't really *run*.
They walked, with packs and bags.

As soon as they got there, down went
the bags, and into the sea they jumped,
swimming and splashing.

Then they looked for shells and seaweed.
They dug holes in the sand and played ball.
They ran up a sand hill
and rolled down
the other side.

When night came, they found firewood.
Mom made a fire.
John and Ann cooked sausages.
And Dad got out some bread and butter.

They sat around the fire and ate
with their fingers.

"These sausages are good," said Dad.
"They're more than good.
They're the best sausages I've ever had."

After supper they sat by the fire,
singing songs. The stars came out.
The moon made a white path on the water.
They could hear the waves
breaking on the beach.

Then it was time for bed.
They put their sleeping bags by the fire
and climbed into them.

Mom lay back, looking at the stars.
"This is lovely," she said.
"I could stay here forever."

"We'll have to go back tomorrow," said Dad.

"Oh, no!" cried John and Ann. "No, Dad."

"You've got school on Monday," Dad said, "and Mom and I have to go to work."

The children grumbled. So did Mom.

"But we'll come back," said Dad.

"When?" asked Ann.

"Let's run away again next Saturday," said Dad, and they all laughed.

Dad rolled over.
"Goodnight," he said.

Possums in a Cherry Tree

If a possum
Met a possum
In a cherry tree,
Should a possum
Ask a possum
Home to have some tea?

Should a possum
Tease a possum?
Would it be unkind?
Should he toss 'im
In the blossom?
Would a possum mind?

How the Turtle Got His Shell

Once upon a time, the turtle had no shell.
His body was soft, like yours and mine.

King Savasi wanted to catch that turtle.
He tried and tried, but the turtle
always got away.

One day, when the turtle was in the sea,
King Savasi called to him.

"Dear turtle," he said,
"don't let us fight like this.
Only children fight. Not turtles and kings.
Look. I'm going to have a big feast.
You must come to it."

"No, thank you," said the turtle.

"Please," said the king.
"It won't be a good feast if you're not there."

"Oh, all right," said the turtle. "I'll come."

On the day of the feast,
the turtle climbed out of the sea
and went to the king's house.

He saw a big pot on the fire.
He saw dishes, but no food.
He saw King Savasi and his men
all looking at him with greedy eyes.

"Well," said the turtle,
"I'm here, but where is the feast?

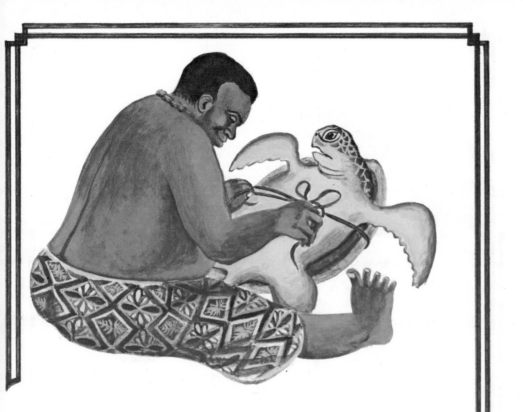

"*You* are the feast!" yelled King Savasi.

He grabbed the turtle and tied him to a dish.

"Now I've got you," laughed the king.
"I'm going to cook you in that pot.
Then I'm going to eat you.
What a lovely feast you will make."

"Oh, no, I won't," said the turtle.
He rolled over and ran away,
the dish tied to his back.

"After him! Catch him!" the king yelled.

Too late. With a splash, the turtle jumped into the sea. He swam and swam, until he was far away from the greedy king.

But the dish
stayed on his back.
And it is still there.